INTRODUCTION By the Author

I was born in Carr Vale, near Bolsover and spent my childhood there since the 1950s. Much has changed even in that short period of time, but the town of Bolsover itself has a fascinating and varied history.

One does not always appreciate the wonders on the doorstep. Take the castle for instance, a magnificent 17th century luxury dwelling. I have seen it most days for almost 60 years and after a while it fades into part of the landscape, whereas visitors marvel at its beauty.

*Apparently many residents were un-aware of how famous the town was centuries ago for producing the finest buckles and clay pipes in Europe. Bolsover **was** on the map even though it was competing with the likes of Chesterfield and Mansfield. Time has taken its toll on the town but its mysteries and charm still abound if you know where to look.*

Several books have been created about Bolsover, many outstanding works from extremely professional historians. Photographs of what was and what is now, have made compelling additions to book shelves.

But what I have tried to accomplish in this portrayal of my home town, is simply its history in one publication, and moving away from the 'text book' approach as in many historical journals.

This is the history of Bolsover through the eyes of a 'Boza' lad, please enjoy it and I hope it will enlighten your interest in our town.

Many thanks

Stuart Haywood

CONTENTS

Page   Chapter

3   BEGINNINGS
7   SAXONS
11   THE CASTLE
17   THE CAVENDISH FAMILY
29   RELIGION AND EDUCATION
32   THE CHAPEL IN THE CASTLE
33   NON-CONFORMATY IN BOLSOVER
35   EDUCATION
38   LANCASHIRE, DERBYSHIRE AND EAST COAST RAILWAY
43   1910 ACCIDENT AT CARR VALE
45   1923 ACCIDENT AT CARR VALE
46   THE MIDLAND RAILWAY
49   COAL MINING IN BOLSOVER
57   ERASIPTERON BOLSOVERI
58   THE END OF COAL MINING
60   SUTTON SCARSDALE
65   OXCROFT SETTLEMENTS
69   HALIFAX BOMBER CRASH 1944
73   PETER FIDLER
77   THE KNIGHTS HOPITALLER
78   THE CHANGING FACE OF BOLSOVER
85   AND FINALLY

BEGINNINGS

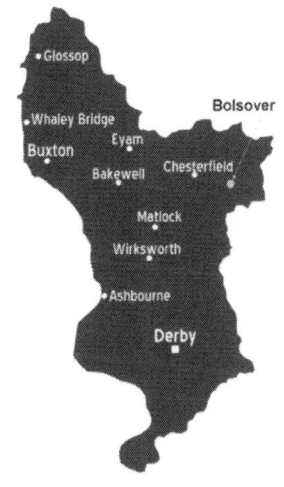

Map of present day Derbyshire

The town of Bolsover in Derbyshire, England, stands on a Magnesium Limestone ridge. There is evidence of habitation in the area as long ago as the Lower Palaeolithic Age with the discovery of a 'stone hand axe' dated to a period of over 120,000 years ago.

The Middle Palaeolithic or (Neanderthal) age between 45,000 and 120,000 years, has produced many finds in the area around Bolsover, as has the Upper Palaeolithic (8,000 to 45,000 years).

It is known that hunters covered vast distances, some from as far away as Holland, Belgium and Germany. They would walk over what is now known as 'Doggerland'. This was a land mass joining England to mainland Europe, but is now under the North Sea.

They would proceed inland, and pass through Creswell Crags and Bolsover as they followed the reindeer into the Derbyshire Peak District.

Flint tools and the evidence of a camp dating back approximately 4500 years were discovered in the 1980s, at Mill Farm, Whaley to the east of Bolsover.

Creswell Crags, *(home to Britain's only known Palaeolithic cave art)* to the east has produced an amazing record of life throughout much of that period. Evidence has also been discovered, proving the existence of people visiting or living in the Bolsover area, from over 120,000 years ago, until present day.

Earthworks are still visible around Bolsover. Two very distinct ones are in a small park called The 'Hornscroft' to the south east of the town, and an area known as The Dykes to the north east. These earthworks were so well constructed, that centuries later they would still be used as fortifications for the town.

There are several theories as to how Bolsover acquired its name. The most popular is that it was named after a person. In the late 8th century, the Vikings or Norsemen began raiding what is now Great Britain. They were hugely successful, and many simply kept what land and possessions they had taken, and subsequently settled on that land. One such warrior was believed to be *Bol* or *Bal*. He had obviously seen the potential of this area as a tenable stronghold. The ridge overlooks the valley below, which runs roughly north west to south east. The monument at Crich can be seen clearly beyond the valley some 48 kilometres away.

Norse Warrior

The high ground is relatively flat, and stretches away to the east, enabling it to be easily defended. The area was known in ancient times as an *'ofer'* . The word 'ofer' describing a ridge or high place. Therefore the name *'Bol'sofer'* was brought about as it was Bol's Ridge or Bol's High Place. But over time the name became Bolsover.

For some unknown reason, however, in the Domesday Book of 1086, it was known as Belesovre, and then changed to Bolsouer in the 1650s.

Still working on the theory of our Norseman 'Bol', archeologists and certain historians believe the name derives from the word, *'Sovre'* also meaning 'high place' or 'settlement'.

So once again this could be *Bolsovre* or 'Settlement of Bol'. The word 'sovre' could quite easily have morphed into 'sover' over time.

Also another lesser known theory, this time away from Norse warriors, and in some respects more feasible, is in the way the ancient people of Bolsover worshipped. If we look at the spelling in the domesday book of 'Belesovre' then it could possibly mean 'Settlement of *Bel*' and not Bol. The word or name 'Bel' has its origins with the Babylonians. Some say they were false gods as the Babylonians had so many it was hard to keep track of them. Bel, though, in this case more than likely translates to 'lord' or 'master'.

It is also believed that the people of Bolsover built a pagan temple, possibly where the Parish Church is now. This belief however cannot be verified due to extensive building on the site over the centuries. This theory is that Iron Age People worshipped either the god 'Bel' as a god in its own right, ie the god of fire perhaps, because at that time metal working and smelting was prominent in the area. Or simply meaning lord or master, therefore is creating the name, 'settlement of Bel' and eventually Belesovre as in the 1086 spelling.

It is highly unlikely at any time in the future that the true meaning of the word Bolsover will be revealed. The town is now called Bolsover however it came into being.

The Romans were believed to have occupied Bolsover, as once again evidence has been discovered. In the Sherwood Lodge area *(see fig 1)* off Hilltop, it is thought a Romano – British structure was constructed, which may have looked something like the drawing *(see fig 2)*.

5

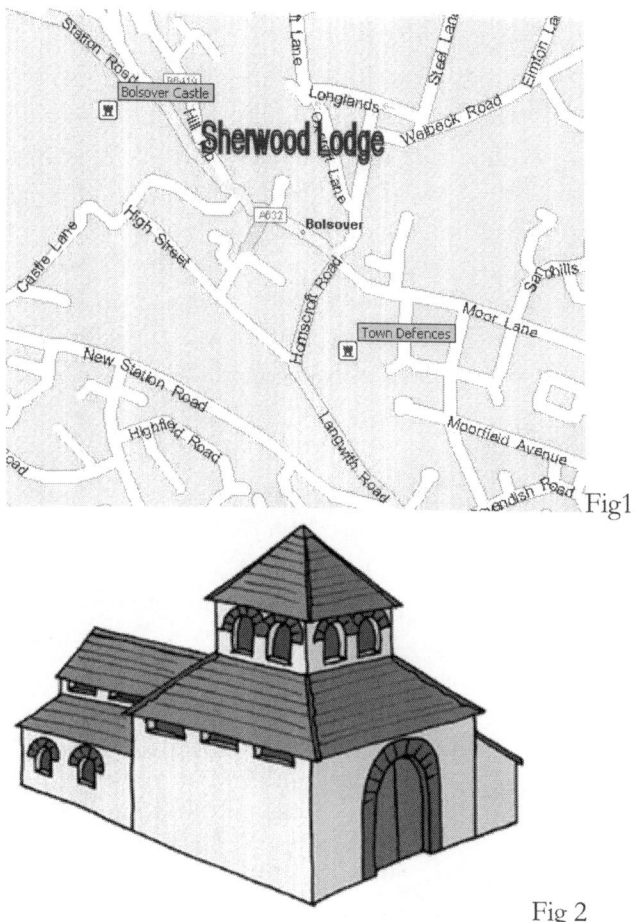

Fig 1

Fig 2

It was used for iron smelting and associated industries. It would seem Bolsover has a long history in metalwork.

THE SAXONS

There has been little or no mention of Bolsover in the official Saxon documents. Until the Norman Conquest after the battle of Hastings in 1066, Bolsover was in the Earldom of Mercia *(see fig 3)*

Fig 3

Leofric, son of Osmund was listed as the Lord of the Hundred of Scarsdale. There were actually 71 places in the Hundred of Scarsdale. It covered a vast area of what is now South Yorkshire and Derbyshire. Leofric also ruled over lands in the Hundred of Stanbridge near Luton in Bedfordshire which only had ten places

His overlord at the time was King Alfred. Leofric was a wealthy landowner and was accredited with considerable lands. In the Domesday Book he was stated to own 3 carucates of land assessed to the geld at Bolsover.

A carucate *(see fig 4)*, was an area of land which was used in Danelaw to assess the amount of tax an individual paid on his land. It was an area of land on which a team of 8 oxen could plough in one season.

Fig 4

7

The carucate was sub divided into oxgangs or bovates which was the area that **one** ox could plough in a season, which in modern Measurements, is about 15 acres. Two oxen would be a vigrate or around 30 acres, up to the carucate which was around 120 acres. Therefore in 1086, Loefric would have owned around 360 acres of farm land. He also had 8 acres of meadow and 2 acres of woodland.

The total population of Bolsover at that time was 17 households, but as this was counted in heads of families only, it would be safe to conclude there would have been around 80 people living here at that time.

After the Norman Conquest, Leofric, as with most Saxon Lords forfeited all their lands to William of Normandy.

Robert of Herils took over as Lord of Scarsdale which included Bolsover. He was appointed Sherriff of Nottinghamshire and Derbyshire by William Peverel. Nothing is known of the Saxon Leofric after his lands had been taken, whether he was banished or he simply disappeared was never documented.

William Peverel was reputed to be the illegitimate son of William 1 of England, otherwise known as William the Conqueror. His mother is said to be a Saxon Princess called Maud Ingelrica, but no written records have ever been found. The name Peverel, has several different spellings. Peverell, Piperell and even Piperellus have all been used over the centuries.

He was given vast lands and wealth by the King, another fact that carried weight to the illegitimate son theory.

He was overlord of a great deal of the English midlands, including of course Bolsover. Peverel immediately set about building castles throughout the Honour of Peverel, as his estates were collectively known. Although no remains or physical evidence has survived in Bolsover, it is generally believed he did in fact build a castle on the site of the later 17th century building, which still stands today in all its splendour overlooking the valley.

This earlier structure would probably have been the same design as 'Peverel Castle' near Castleton in the Peak District. *(see fig 5)*. Although now a ruin, it clearly shows the Norman style of keep.

Fig 5

Bolsover, according to the Domesday Book, was worth £2 in 1066, and in 1086 had risen to the princely sum of £3
William Peverel the Elder frequently gets confused with his son William Peverel the Younger. William the Elder died in Nottingham in 1115 and William the Younger inherited the Honour of Peverel which included Bolsover.
Henry 1 of England became king in August 1100 after several skirmishes with his brothers. When Henry died in 1135, a squabble broke out between his daughter Empress Matilda and his nephew Stephen of Blois. So the 'Anarchy' or 'Chaos' as it was also known began. This was one of England's many civil wars throughout the ages.

Both wanted the throne. Stephen had crossed the channel with his brother and quickly claimed the vacant throne. This was due to Henry's eldest son and true heir, William Adelin, drowning in the sinking of 'The White Ship' in 1120.

Eventually after years of fighting, Empress Matilda went to Normandy and let her son Henry Fitzempress continue with the war against Stephen. Throughout this time, William Peverel the Younger supported Stephen with money and fighting men.

Stephen was finally forced to sign a treaty in 1153 called the 'Treaty of Wallingford', after nearly fifteen years of fighting.

Henry II (Matilda's son), became king of England in 1154. He had not forgotten those who had fought and plotted against his mother Matilda, so he began seeking them out for retribution but seems to have stopped short of actual murder. For fear of reprisals though, and perhaps starting more conflicts, he decided to 'remove' his old enemies by other means.

William Peverel the Younger was certainly on his to do list. Promptly, Peverel was accused of trying to poison Ranulf de Gernon, 4th Earl of Chester the previous year.
Records do state that Peverel did, in fact poison de Gernon at a banquet held in his honour. Some of Gernon's aides died and he was violently ill. On hearing about it, the king promptly took this opportunity of stripping Peverel of all his lands and wealth and giving them to the unfortunate Gernon.
Poisoned or not, Gernon did in actual fact die before he could take possession of the Honour of Peverel. His son Hugh de Kevelioc, 5th Earl of Chester inherited his father's wealth at the tender age of six.

As he was well under age, basically Bolsover and its manors were now owned by the crown. It stayed that way until Richard 1st *(Richard the Lionheart)* gave Bolsover to his Brother Prince John in 1189.

In 1194, after John's rebellion, Bolsover reverted once again into the possession of the Crown. Several Governors and Constables were appointed to oversee Bolsover. In 1216 the King transferred custody of the castle to William de Ferrars, Earl of Derby.
The existing Constable at the time was Gerard de Furnival who was not about to relinquish Bolsover without a fight. Ferrers besieged the castle and took it by force.
Ferrers spent the next seven years repairing the damage to the castle. In 1223, the first of the 'new towers' had been built. Five years later the second had been completed.

A succession of Dukes and Earls were given the manor over the years until it once again reverted to the crown in 1547.
In 1553 it was granted to Sir George Talbot. *(see fig 6)*

Fig 6 Sir George Talbot

THE CASTLE

THE CASTLE AND THE CAVENDISH FAMILY
The 'castle' itself has been the subject of several publications over the years; therefore its history will be summarized briefly in this chapter.

As previously stated there was a building on the site of the existing 'castle'. This was most likely built in the 11th and 12th centuries, as no mention of a large structure was mentioned in the Domesday Book.

Also in the building accounts of work undertaken by Cavendish in constructing the present 'castle', it stated monies had been paid out for 'demolition of the **older buildings**'. This indicates clearly, that some type of construction had previously been built on the site.

In 1560 Sir George Talbot *(see fig 6 previous page)* succeeded his father and became the 6th Earl of Shrewsbury and one of the richest men in England. George died in 1590 and his estate went to his son Gilbert *(see fig 7)* who was the 7th Earl. He grew up with, and became a close friend of Charles Cavendish *(see fig 8)* and in 1608, 'leased' Bolsover to Charles for a thousand years at £10 per year.

Cavendish later bought the castle outright and began work on converting the old 'Norman' castle into a residence. He employed the services of Robert Smithson or (Smythson) as his designer, who

Fig 7   Fig 8   designed much of Hardwick Hall for his mother 'Bess of Hardwick'. Charles had a vision; he was very much like his mother in the fact they both had an affinity for building grand residences. Unfortunately Charles and Smithson both died before the building work had progressed very far.

The designs for the 'castle' seem to have been produced in two distinct styles.

Firstly the poetic and romantic dream that is the little castle, or 'keep' *(see fig 9)* as some call it, then the splendour and materialism of the time, portrayed in the terrace *(see fig 10)*. It was luxurious architecture befitting a very wealthy individual.

Fig 9. The Little Castle

Fig 10 The Terrace

Materials for the construction were sourced locally. The stone came from the Shuttlewood, Bolsover Moor and Bolsover Town quarries. This was supplemented by using second hand stone from other buildings, mainly a building in Kirkby in Ashfield.

Timber was from Scarcliffe Park and lime was burnt in kilns close to the site.

Charles' son William Cavendish, *(see fig 11)* together with Robert's son John Smithson *(At that time the spelling of the family name was Smythson, it was not until the next generation that Smithson was adopted)*, carried on what their fathers' had begun.

Fig 11

Around 1630 the residence was ready for occupancy. Water was piped in through a series of **'Conduit' Houses'** *(see fig 12)* enabling a fresh supply of running water to the site.

Fig 12 Cundy House (Also known as a Conduit House)

13

On 30th July 1634, Sir William Cavendish, who was now Earl of Newcastle, hosted a great banquet at Bolsover for King Charles 1st and his Queen, Henrietta Maria. Ben Jonson *(see fig 13)*, the famous renaissance dramatist, Poet and Author was commissioned to produce entertainment for the evening. He wrote and performed a '**Masque**' entitled '**Loves Welcome to Bolsover**'. The banquet was a lavish affair and was reported to cost what would be in excess of £1m today.

It was held in the great hall which ran almost the length of the terrace. The meal was said to have included some 48 different birds.

Fig 13 Ben Jonson

William Cavendish decided that a new and sophisticated approach to design would be needed. He was loyal to John Smithson and waited until he had completed what had been asked of him before employing his son Huntingdon Smithson. As a superb horseman, Cavendish felt the residence was incomplete without a state of the art riding centre.

Huntingdon carried out the work on the riding school, also the boundary wall enclosing the great hall, and both the south east and south west gates.

As Cavendish was a Royalist, and fought for the King (Charles l). In August 1644, the garrison at Bolsover was attacked and accepted the surrender terms of the Parliamentary forces under Colonel Muschamp. The Royalist troops were allowed to leave Bolsover. Cavendish was not at Bolsover at that time, he was campaigning and fighting further north with Prince Rupert.

A report at the time stated:

"They marched out with drums and colours, horses, swords and pistols, leaving behind them 'six pieces of ordnance and three hundred firearms', the castle and manor being sequestrated"

The castle was then garrisoned by the Parliamentary forces until 1649 when the *'Trustees of Delinquents' Estates'* ordered the Committee of Derbyshire to demolish the outer works and garden walls, and basically any structure which could be used in the defense of the castle. Even the huge doors were removed and smaller ones fitted. (Evidence of the original hinges etc. can still be seen around the 'little castle'.)

When William Cavendish returned from the continent after he had been granted his possessions, he found the castle in a terrible state. The occupying Parliamentary forces had looted and ransacked it. All his works of art and anything of value had been stripped.
The building itself had begun to show signs of decay. In some cases demolition work had begun not only in the outer buildings but the 'little castle' itself.

In many ways it must have been a sad and daunting task, but William set about the rebuilding and employed the services of a Bolsover Mason called Joseph Jackson contracted under the agent Andrew Clayton.

The Gallery roof had been stripped of most of its lead and for five years very little progress was made, showing how much damage had been inflicted at Bolsover.
Money was not too forthcoming also at that time for William. The war and his allegiance with the crown had cost him dearly. Some reports have his debts at almost £1m. In the 17th century, that amount of money was astronomical.

In a letter from his agent Andrew Clayton, the agent states that the roof was ready but he was unable to purchase the lead until further rents came in. It was all a little hand to mouth.
William, however, persevered and began slowly to resurrect the 'castle'.

Six years after the castle had been restored, William sadly died on Christmas Day 1676. He had reached the grand old age of 84, a rarity in the 17th century. He was buried in Westminster Abbey.

His son, Henry succeeded him as 2nd Duke of Newcastle and the owner of Bolsover Castle.

In 1691, after the death of Henry, the title became extinct. He had no sons so his estate went to his daughter Lady Margaret Cavendish.

Subsequent heredity did keep the 'castle' in a state of repair until Lady Henrietta Cavendish Holles, Countess of Oxford stripped the roof from the terrace and other building materials for use at Welbeck Abbey in the mid seventeen hundreds.
The castle slowly went into decline and in 1945 the 7th Duke of Portland gave Bolsover Castle to the then Ministry of Works (Department of Environment).
The castle is now in the hands of English Heritage.

THE CAVENDISH FAMILY

The Cavendish family history dates back several hundred years, however, this account begins with the Rt. Hon William Cavendish *(see fig 14)* born in 1505. He married three times, his first two marriages were to Margaret Bostock who bore him five children, but only two daughters survived. Margaret died in 1540. He then married Elizabeth Parker in 1542.

Elizabeth had no surviving children and died during childbirth in 1546. The baby was stillborn.

In 1547 he married for the third time to the 26 year old Elizabeth Barlow *(see fig 15)*

Fig 14

. This was Elizabeth's second marriage. Her first was to Robert Barlow who at the time was only 13 years of age. Barlow was a sickly young man and the marriage was never consummated. He died in 1535 leaving Elizabeth a wealthy woman.

With her marriage to William she now became Lady Cavendish. She was born Elizabeth Hardwick to John Hardwick and Elizabeth Leake. She was better known throughout the ages as 'Bess of Hardwick'

Fig 15

17

The couple had eight children in all, but two died in infancy.

Frances Cavendish (18 June 1548 - January 1632)

Temperance Cavendish (10 June 1549 - 1550), died in infancy.

Henry Cavendish (17 December 1550 - 28 October 1616)

William Cavendish (27 December 1552 – 3 March 1626)

Charles Cavendish (28 November 1553 - 4 April 1617)

Elizabeth Cavendish (31 March 1555 – 21 January 1582)

Mary Cavendish (January 1556 - April 1632)

Lucrece Cavendish (born and died 1556), probably the twin of Mary.

In 1552 the couple began to build Chatsworth House after William had purchased the estate three years previous.

William Cavendish died in 1557 and his eldest son Henry succeeded his titles.

Elizabeth married once again in 1559. Her third husband was Sir William St. Loe and she became Lady St Loe.

When St Loe died in 1564/5 he had no male heirs and left everything to Elizabeth. There were questions raised at the time as to the manner of his death. It was widely believed that he was in fact, poisoned by his brother. But his brother inherited nothing as did William's two daughters.

Elizabeth was now an extremely wealthy woman; she had a yearly income of around £60,000. As of 2013, that equates to almost £16m. She was still only in her late 30s and had kept her health and good looks. Several men courted her but she remained single until 1568 when she married George Talbot, 6th Earl of Shrewsbury *(see fig 6)* to become Countess of Shrewsbury.

George had seven children from his first marriage, and with the six children of Elizabeth, the house hold was becoming rather busy.

There was a double wedding ceremony in February 1568 when Elizabeth's daughter Mary Cavendish aged 12 was given to marriage with George's son Gilbert who was 16.

Also Elizabeth's son Sir Henry Cavendish aged 18 married George's daughter Lady Grace Talbot who was only 8 years old. Talbot had been given the unenviable task as Jailor to Mary Queen of Scots *(see fig 16)*. This did, in many respects put a strain on the marriage.

Fig 16

They were allowed £2500 per year by Queen Elizabeth I *(see fig 17)* to 'keep' Mary, but the figure actually spent was nearer to £10,000. This financial burden was probably one of the major factors in their separation.

Even Queen Elizabeth tried on several occasions to reunite them without success. Certain records and accounts state that Mary Queen of Scots herself was instrumental in their problems compounding them greatly by inferring that George and she were having a relationship. This had never been proved, but it would undoubtedly diminish the trust and love she had for George. He died in November 1590.

Fig 17 Queen Elizabeth I

19

Elizabeth 'Bess of Hardwick' died in 1608, and was well into her eighties. The couple never had children.

Elizabeth's son Charles (*see fig 8*), and Talbot's son Gilbert (*see fig 7*) grew up as friends, step brothers and brothers in law. Charles showed an interest in Bolsover Castle and the site. Which at that time would probably have been the ruins of the earlier fortress built by the Normans.

Charles took it on a lease from Gilbert of £10.00 per year for 1,000 years. He seemed to have the same passion for building as his mother and soon began work on the property. *(see previous chapter)*

Charles married Catherine Ogle suo Jure, Baroness Ogle on 11th July 1591. December 1593 saw the birth of a son, William. Charles and Catherine had three sons but one died in infancy leaving William to grow up with his younger brother Charles.

WILLIAM CAVENDISH (1st Duke of Newcastle)

William's father Charles died in 1617 and his mother urged him to marry as soon as possible.

William did, and in October 1618 he married the nineteen year old Elizabeth Bassett who had been widowed two years previous. They had several children during their marriage.

Six sons were born but only two survived to adulthood, and four daughters, one who also died young.

His busy lifestyle included an education at St John's College Cambridge. He still found time, however, to oversee the building of the residence at Bolsover following the legacy of his father.

It is said by some that his time spent at St John's was not best used, as he was more interested in sports such as, horse riding and swordsmanship, rather than academics.

William became close friends with King Charles 1st and his Queen Henrietta Maria *(see fig 18)*, and in 1638 accepted the post of Governor to the King's eldest son Prince Charles, who would later become King Charles 2nd.

In 1639, William Cavendish actually lent the King £10,000 to help with his efforts in suppressing various revolts including the Scottish. He also raised an army for him which he would lead into battle himself.

Fig 18 Charles I and Queen Henrietta

Much is written about William Cavendish 1st Duke of Newcastle and the English Civil War. Therefore this account will commence after the Duke resigned his commission and fled to Europe following the defeat at Marston Moor in July 1644.

He arrived in Hamburg after several days at sea. He had travelled with his brother Charles and his two sons Charles and Henry. Both his sons had taken ill on the voyage but fortunately recovered.

He had less than £100 with him and knew he would need credit. With money at his disposal, he made his way to Paris and immediately presented himself to Queen Henrietta Maria.

His fist wife Elizabeth died in childbirth on April 17th 1643 during his campaigns. The couple had a close and loving relationship which left him devastated. He took leave from the battlefield to attend her funeral service.

Once at the court of the Queen, he was to meet his second wife, Margaret Lucas *(see fig 19)*. She was the youngest of eight children born to wealthy land owner Sir Thomas Lucas. The couple were married at Sir Richard Browne's Chapel in Paris in 1645.

Margaret was an author, poet, dramatist, philosopher and 'natural scientist'. She wrote several accounts of William's life. One in particular is called 'The Cavalier in Exile' portraying their life together during that period. Margaret was known at the time as 'Mad Madge of Newcastle'

Fig 19 Margaret Lucas

Even Samuel Pepys referred to her as 'Mad, conceited and ridiculous.' William and Margaret were basically penniless and living on credit. They moved into the house once owned by the widow of the artist, Peter Paul Rubens, in Antwerp. A short excerpt from an essay by Margaret shows the simplicity of the life they had become accustomed to.

She writes:

"Howsoever our fortunes are, we are both content, spending our time harmlessly. For my Lord pleaseth himself with the management of some few horses, and exercises himself with the use of the sword; which two arts he hath brought by his studious thoughts, rational experience and industrious practice to an absolute perfection . "

William realised he would have to address his finances as credit would have to be paid back someday. He was labeled a 'Delinquent' by Parliament. This was a name given to Loyalists after the Civil War ended.

To reclaim his estates, as they had been sequestrated by Parliament, he would be required to 'compound himself,' basically apologise and pay a fine. His brother Charles went to England on his behalf to negotiate with Parliament.

Charles too, would have to pay for his estates. At first they told him he could have his estates restored for a fee of £4,500. But

Parliament then decided to re-evaluate his properties and demanded another £500. He had no choice but to sell some properties to raise the money. Soon after, Charles became ill and never recovered. Sadly he died in 1654 at the age of 63. William was once again devastated as the two brothers had been extremely close throughout their lives.

William returned to England to find Bolsover in a ruinous condition. He died on Christmas Day 1676 aged 84. Unlike other Cavendish members who are entombed in the Church in Bolsover, his tomb is in Westminster Abbey.

He was succeeded by his only son Henry Cavendish 2nd Duke of Newcastle. *(see fig 20)*

Henry, who was previously Viscount Mansfield, became the 2nd Duke of Newcastle upon William's death. Below is a time line of some of the honours bestowed on his father William Cavendish 1st Duke of Newcastle.

1614   MP for East Retford

1620   Granted Viscount Mansfield by James 1st

1625   Lord Lieutenant of Nottinghamshire

1627   1st Baron Cavendish of Bolsover

1628   Lord Lieutenant of Derbyshire

1628   1st Earl of Newcastle by Charles 1st

1629   9th Baron of Ogle

1643   1st Marques of Newcastle

1649   Knighted and Order of the Garter

1664   1st Duke of Newcastle.

Henry Cavendish 2nd Duke of Newcastle
(24 June 1630 - 26 July 1691)

Fig 20 Henry Cavendish

Henry was the younger of the two surviving sons of William and Elizabeth. His elder brother Charles died in 1659 at the age of thirty two He became the 2nd Duke of Newcastle in 1676 following the death of his father William. He fought with his father during the war and followed him into exile. He returned to England in 1647 in an attempt to help his family recover its estates, including Bolsover.

Following the restoration, he decided to go into politics and became M.P. for Derbyshire and then Northumberland. He was also a privy councillor as well as the governor of Berwick upon Tweed. His titles also included; Lord Lieutenant of the counties of Northumberland, Nottinghamshire and the then three ridings of Yorkshire. After the accession of *William and Mary (See below)*, Henry resigned all his appointments and refused to take oaths to the new King

William and Mary:

In 1689 Parliament declared that King James had abdicated by deserting his Kingdom. The throne was offered jointly to William III and Mary II. Mary reigned until 1694 and William until 1702. This action seemed to be, by many, a way of ensuring the Monarchy would not interfere with the decisions of Parliament. It was less than popular with many, including Henry Cavendish who still regarded the Monarchy.

Henry basically retired from public life and lived at Welbeck where his only son died. In the absence of a male heir, Henry left his estates to his third daughter Lady Margaret Cavendish. *(see fig 21)*

Fig 21 Lady Margaret Cavendish

Margaret married John Holles *(see fig 22)* in 1691. Holles was granted the title of, 1st Duke of Newcastle as the title had become extinct with the death of Henry 2nd Duke of Newcastle and no male heir. Therefore it was a second creation of the title proudly held by her grandfather William. *(In some historical documentation the title is also referred to as '3rd Duke of Newcastle')*

Fig 22 John Holles

Holles and Margaret had just the one child, Lady Henrietta Cavendish Holles *(see fig 23)* born in 1694. Henry Cavendish was, although retired, a very powerful man with renowned connections. Because of her father, Henrietta's hand was sought in marriage even in her youth. She courted many Dukes, Earls, Lords and other nobility. Her father finally chose Edward Harley, *(see fig 24)* 2nd Earl of Oxford and Earl Mortimer. Henrietta and Edward were married in 1713 and had two children, Henry, who died in infancy and Margaret Cavendish Harley. Edward Harley immediately inherited the Cavendish estates including Bolsover, Welbeck and Wimpole Hall in Cambridgeshire. Although Wimpole was their main residence, they had to sell it in 1740 to pay Harley's debts.

Fig 23 Lady Henrietta Cavendish

25

Bolsover was becoming a less interesting proposition for the family and it began to suffer the indignity of lack of maintenance. Harley died in June 1741 and is buried in the vault of the Duke of Newcastle in Westminster Abbey.

Fig 24 Edward Harley

Henrietta died in 1755 and is buried next to her husband.

MARGARET CAVENDISH HARLEY, *(see fig 25)* the daughter of Henrietta and Edward was their sole heir. She was also believed to be the four times great granddaughter of Queen Elizabeth I on her mother's side. She was twenty years of age when she married William Bentinck, 2nd Duke of Portland *(see fig 26)* on July 11th 1734 at Oxford Chapel, Marylebone.

Fig 25 Margaret Cavendish Bentinck

The marriage produced six children all of who were born at Welbeck.

Fig 26 William Bentinck, 2nd Duke of Portland

Of the six children, two were sons, William Henry Cavendish-Bentinck who was born in April 1738, and Lord Edward Charles Cavendish-Bentinck born in March 1744.

26

Edward went on to have a career as a Member of Parliament for several different constituencies, but his older brother William not only inherited the estates of his parents, but his career in politics actually took him to 10 Downing Street as Prime Minister of the United Kingdom, *(see fig 27)* not once but twice. His first office was from April to December 1783, then a longer term from March 1807 to October 1809 as a member of the Whigs, later the Tory party.

Fig 27 above right and left
William Henry Cavendish-Bentinck Prime Minister and 3rd Duke of Portland

William's mother Margaret died in 1785. She had a great interest in fine art and natural history. During her life she amassed the largest collection in Britain. After her death the collection was sold off in 1786 with the sale lasting 38 days due to the vast amount of items. One of the most famous items in Margaret's possession was the 'Portland Vase'. *(Right)* The vase was loaned to Josiah Wedgwood who painstakingly endeavoured to produce a copy. The vase is now in the British Museum.

Following two brief marriages, William Henry married Lady Dorothy Cavendish *(see fig 28)* in 1766. Dorothy was the daughter of

27

 William Cavendish, 4th Duke of Devonshire, and Charlotte Cavendish, Marchioness of Hartington.

Fig 28 Lady Dorothy Cavendish

William Henry's eldest son, also William Henry, inherited his father's titles and became the 4th Duke of Portland. Successive Dukes followed until 1990 when the 9th Duke of Portland, His Grace Victor Frederick William Cavendish-Bentinck died without an heir and the Dukedom became extinct. Bolsover Castle had already been given by the 7th Duke in 1945 to the Ministry of Works, later called the Department of the Environment, and as of 2013 is in the ownership of English Heritage.

Bolsover Castle was abandoned as a residence in favour of Welbeck throughout the early eighteenth century. Succeeding generations of the Dukes of Portland contributed little to maintain the building. Far from it as even part of the roof and other building materials were taken to be used at Welbeck. But extensive restoration work has been ongoing for several years and much of the grand building has been returned to its former glory.

RELIGION AND EDUCATION

As stated previously, it was thought that the people of Bolsover built a pagan temple for worship on the site of the present St Mary and St Laurence Church on high street, known locally as the Parish Church.

It has even been suggested that the temple may have been on the site of the castle itself. This would perhaps be more logical as it offers a commanding view overlooking the valley.

Wherever it was, no archaeology has been discovered to confirm either claim. The god 'Bel' referred to earlier could, in this context be a derivative of the Phoenician god of fire, as archaeologists have found evidence that Bolsover was heavily involved in the smelting of both lead and tin. Large post holes have been discovered around the area denoting large, permanent buildings were erected as early foundries.

Also with permanent structures, there tended to be temples for worship, which lends further credibility to the theory that such a place would have been used in Bolsover.

Although once again no archaeological proof has been found, Bolsover was said to have had a Saxon Church in 656. This belief has been strengthened with the discovery of a Saxon Church at Ault Hucknall a few kilometers to the west of Bolsover, and at Sutton Scarsdale across the valley. As many Saxon Churches were predominantly made of wood, very little has survived over time. Perhaps the church in Bolsover may have looked similar to *Fig 29*

Fig 29 Saxon Church

29

The present church on High Street consists of stonework from the Normans shortly after 1066. The tower with its arched doorway is typical of the period. Extensions and modifications continued throughout the coming years, culminating in the addition around 1618 of the Cavendish Chapel. Inside the church is a rare stone engraving known as 'The Manger of Bethlehem'. *(see fig 30)*
The piece dates to around AD1300 when it was said to have been given to the church.

Fig 30
The Manger of Bethlehem

It was so highly treasured, that when news of the impending Parliamentary forces attack reached Bolsover, it was buried face down near the Priest's doorway to save it from theft or damage. This did not seem to be the case however, as no records of any damage or thefts from the church were found. It was later taken out and replaced in the church. Accounts later revealed that the ancient 'Church Plate' and the bells did find their way into the Parliamentarian's 'booty bags' more than likely to be smelted down.

In January 1897 a fire broke out in the vestry twenty years after the church had undergone major restorations costing in excess of £5,000.
The interior was severely damaged including the clocks and bells. Restoration began once more including new seats and a new organ, this time the cost was £10,000. It was reopened in September 1898.

The church suffered another fire in 1960 and was again restored, this time at a cost of £70,000.

Bolsover Church of St Mary and St. Lawrence (Laurence)

Between 1867 and 1900, the vicar of Bolsover was the Revd T.C. Hills. Revd Hills was also the first chairman of the urban district council. He gave his name to Hillstown.

THE CHAPEL IN THE CASTLE

It has been recorded that in 1220 (The date cannot be confirmed), William Ferrers, Earl of Derby granted Darley Abbey 1 Mark of silver towards funding a chaplain to conduct services in the chapel in the castle.

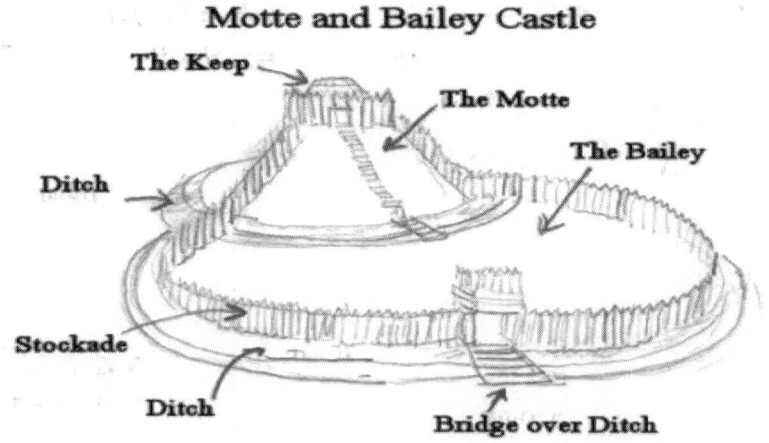

At that time the castle was most likely a motte and bailey construction *(above)*. The 'motte' would be a mound of earth on top of which would be the keep. The bailey was the fortified, enclosed lower section where personnel essential to the running of the castle would live.

The Lord resided in the keep where, it would house the chapel for both convenience and safety.

As the present keep or 'little castle' is probably built on the site of the medieval keep, it has not been possible to excavate, therefore definitive proof has not been found which confirms this was the site of the chapel.
There was no mention of a church in the 'Domesday' entry for Bolsover in 1086, but sometime between 1149 and 1155, William

Peverel the younger was persuaded by his wife to give some land to Darley Abbey in order to establish a church.
The land was described as:

'All that lying between Hanel and Godrichesgrif as far as the river Doe Lea, together with the site of the mill of Botrehalg and Mulnecroft next to the wood.

This land may have been in the Bolsover Woodhouse area and by 1291 consisted of 20 acres.
The first vicarage in Bolsover was ordained in the time of Bishop Alexander Stavensby (1224 - 1238) and in 1291 was valued at £13.6s.8d.

NONCOMFORMITY IN BOLSOVER

Presbyterian meeting house
A building was erected on high street in Bolsover during 1622 and is said to be one of the oldest non-conformist chapel buildings in Derbyshire. This building is now a medical centre; it was the meeting house of the Presbyterian church, a branch of Reformed Protestantism.
It was used for many years as a Presbyterian meeting house and finally closed, to be opened up again as an independent meeting house in 1817.

Bolsover Methodist Church

The Methodist church *(right)* is the latest in a series of churches and meeting houses used by the Methodist church.

33

The first Wesleyan chapel, founded in 1826, stood on the corner of Chapel Breck and Station Road. By the 1860s it was decided that the building was too small for the ever growing congregation and was converted into dwellings. A second chapel was built on Hilltop but was replaced in 1897 by the present Methodist Church.
The second chapel is now in use as a meeting room called 'The Assembly Hall'

A Congregational mission was established in Carr Vale and was opened in 1902. This mission became a separate church in 1936 but continued to share a minister with the Castle Street church.

Several other churches, chapels and meeting houses have been established in Bolsover over the ages. In September 1904 work began in building the first Wesleyan Methodist church in New Bolsover *(see fig 31)*. This was at the junction of Chapel Road and New Station Road. The memorial stones were laid by Emerson Bainbridge.

Fig 31

The church was adjacent to the orphanage for miner's children, which is now known as Bainbridge Hall. The chapel was opened in 1905. The chapel remained in use after the unification of

Methodism but eventually closed in 1979. It was demolished in the early 1990s. A housing development now occupies the site.

The Jehovah's Witnesses were registered in Bolsover in 1997, and subsequently built a new Kingdom Hall on the site of the old Pentecostal church on High Street.

EDUCATION

There seems to be no records of an endowed school in Bolsover before 1751, although a William Armstrong taught at a private school.
Henrietta Harley, Countess of Oxford died in 1755 leaving in her will, £6 per year for a school to be established in Bolsover. In 1756 a school room was built on Castle Street. In 1772 it was teaching six children to read and write. By 1823 this had risen to around fifty pupils, both girls and boys. This may not seem a huge number but until the arrival of the railway and coal mines the population of Bolsover had remained fairly consistent at less than two thousand.
In 1833 a Sunday school at the parish church was said to have 63 boys and 60 girls in attendance. Their fees were paid by the churchwardens.

In 1844 the endowed school became a National school, and during 1845-48 received Education Committee grants totalling £110.
In addition to the school-house near the castle there was an infants' school, plus two private schools.

Further grants in 1868 and 1872, enabled the National school to completely rebuild, adding an infants' room. All fees were finally abolished at the school in 1893. By the turn of the century the population was growing at a rapid rate and the demand for education was greatly increasing. An Inspector of schools called in to the National school and found gross overcrowding. The school was designed for 376 pupils but there were 672 on the books and 545 actually in attendance on that day. He quickly reported back, that at least one thousand extra child places were desperately needed.

By that time the Bolsover Colliery School was established and was allowed to use the large hall for teaching. The situation was so severe that children under eight were removed from the main schools and taught in temporary schools provided by the Methodist chapel in Carr Vale, and the Congregational schoolroom on High Street.

Soon, new schools were built in the surrounding districts as well as Bolsover. Hillstown, Shuttlewood, Palterton, Scarcliffe and many others gratefully received the new buildings.

In 1907 a new infant's school at new Bolsover was completed, and consisted of six classrooms which could accommodate 320 infants. Two other schools built on Welbeck Road were completed the same year. The pressure on the education system was gradually reducing, but staffing problems began to arise especially at the Church of England school. By 1919 the problem had become so acute due to overcrowding and staff shortages that it was reduced to half-time attendance. Things, however did improve and by 1935 it was said to be 'in a very credible state'.

It was decided that a new senior girl's school was needed and building was started and completed in 1939. Because the site was prone to subsidence the materials would be of 'light construction'. So they arranged several 'wooden huts' in terraces.

The latest addition to education in Bolsover is 'The Bolsover School' *(see fig 32)*.

Fig 32 The Bolsover School

The state of the art education facility was up and running in 2010.

LANCASHIRE, DERBYSHIRE AND EAST COAST RAILWAY

William Arkwright, a descendent of Sir Richard Arkwright of Cromford Mill had an idea to link the west and east coasts by rail enabling trade to flourish between the two points. There was an abundance of coal beneath his lands and an independent railway would allow for the rapid distribution of the produce.
In 1887 he proposed the Chesterfield and Lincoln Direct Railway. It was designed to cross his land, as at that time he owned Sutton Scarsdale Hall and estate. It would meet up with the larger Midland Railway at each end.
For some reason his proposal was not met with a great deal of enthusiasm so the idea was shelved. However, this did not deter him, and he continued his ideas for an independent railway running from west to east.
Finally through sheer determination, his endeavours paid off. On 5th August 1891 the Lancashire, Derbyshire and East Coast Railway Act was given the Royal Assent.
The planned route was to be from Warrington, through Knutsford then northwest of Macclesfield on to Buxton and eventually into Chesterfield after negotiating the Derbyshire Peak District.
Upon leaving the Market Place station, it would pass over a 210m viaduct at Horns Bridge and on through Arkwright, Duckmanton and Bolsover. The Bolsover Station would actually be in Carr Vale. From there it would pass through a tunnel some 2,399m long before emerging at Scarcliffe station. Ollerton, Tuxford and Lincoln would be the next ports of call. From Lincoln it would complete the west-east journey and arrive in Sutton-on-Sea in Lincolnshire close to Mablethorpe.
The potential of this route sounded tremendous, not only could he transport goods and coal, he could accommodate miners, railway workers and their families on trips to the seaside.

But lack of investment and the enormous cost of driving a railway through the Peak District caused him to cut back. He needed in the region of £5m for the whole project but could only raise a small percentage of the money. It was decided due to the lack of money that the railway would run from Chesterfield to Lincoln only.

The Logo of the Lancashire, Derbyshire and East Coast Railway Company; it was given the Royal Assent in 1891.

Below is the route of the completed railway. It ran for only 56 miles instead of the intended 170 miles.

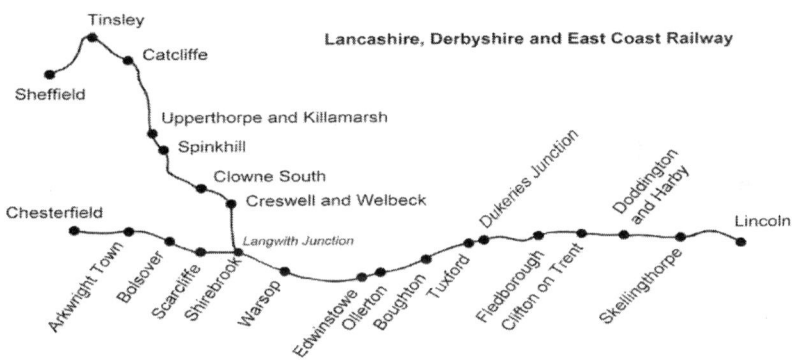

The railway was completed and opened in 1897.
The branch line to Sheffield was completed in 1900.

One claim to fame of this small, but *'very well turned out little railway,'* as it was described at the time, was that on 10th September 1906 it was asked to convey King Edward VII from Ollerton to London. Buckingham Palace 'failed' to mention that the Royal Family was expected to 'pay' for the Royal Train. Whether they did or not has not been substantiated.

Harry Willmott, who had been the General Manager of the Lancashire, Derbyshire and East Coast Railway, had to retire through ill health in 1905. The Great Central Railway took this opportunity and in January 1907 the railway was taken over by them.

The tunnel between the station at Carr Vale and the Scarcliffe station had proved difficult even in its construction. The tunnel workers hit coal deposits and had trouble getting through the magnesium limestone. At one point the contractors, S. Pearson and Son could only progress around 55 metres per week. The finished tunnel was approximately 8 meters wide and 6.3 meters high. The ingress of water was a major factor which was never really resolved. At one point almost 200,000 gallons of water had to be pumped out of the tunnel every day.

A water company was set up which supplied the surrounding area. Another problem was subsidence. Coal, being the very reason for building the railway, was becoming a factor in its demise. By 1951 the tunnel was dangerous and unsafe; concerns were being raised for the safety of passengers. The estimated cost of repairing the tunnel was put at over £1m. This, coupled with the astronomical costs of continued maintenance made the decision to close the tunnel easy.

Previous page: The tunnel from Carr Vale to Scarcliffe, showing a dual line running through. The tracks were later pulled up and a single track re-laid in the centre due to the unstable nature of the tunnel. The tunnel was closed to passenger traffic in December 1951.
At a length of 2.399 meters it was the eighteenth longest tunnel in Great Britain.

In 1966 the Coal Board decided to infill the tunnel with colliery waste using earth moving vehicles. Work began on 10th October 1966 when two Aveling-Barford SL dump trucks *(see fig 33 and 34)*, known by the fitters who worked on them as 'Flying Pigs' began hauling the 115,000 cubic meters needed into the tunnel. Over 400 tons were deposited in the tunnel each day where a mechanical shovel would then compact the material, leaving a one metre gap between the fill and the roof for ventilation.

Fig 33 below,'Flying Pig in tunnel
Fig 34 left, Aveling-Barford SL dump truck, turning in the tight confines of Bolsover tunnel.

At the time of its closure, the line was owned by British Railways. Another contributory factor of the closure was the condition of the viaduct over the Midland Railway line on the approach to the station.

The viaduct was an eight arched brick built structure. It was

almost 23 metres high with a span of over 112 metres. It was said that the viaduct actually swayed and shook as trains ran over it. It was decided to demolish it and in August 1952 several explosive charges were laid. Eye witnesses said that there were loud bangs and clouds of dust. But when the dust settled, the *'unstable and unsafe'* viaduct still stood in all its glory. It was decided to use heavy machinery, and at 8.15 am on Sunday August 24th, the structure was 'pulled' down. The rubble was cleared as quickly as possible in order to minimize the closure of the Midland Line onto which it fell.

RAILWAY DISASTERS

The railway; however was not without incidents through the years. Several accidents occurred with some causing fatalities. Two terrible accidents at the Bolsover station, renamed Bolsover South in September 1950, happened in 1910 and again in 1923.

1910 ACCIDENT AT BOLSOVER STATION

On Saturday 24th December 1910 at around 5.15 pm a passenger train pulled into the station. A group of children had congregated around the wicket gate at the level crossing. A Great Northern coal train pulling empty trucks approached the station and blew its warning whistle. For some reason the children did not respond and the engine tragically ploughed into them.

The train continued on its journey with the driver unaware that a catastrophe had just occurred. The dead and injured were strewn around the crossing. People rushed to their aid and began taking the injured onto the platform.

A doctor by the name of Spencer happened to be on the platform waiting to greet friends when a man approached him carry a child. He immediately commandeered a room next to the booking hall to be use as a make shift medical unit. The young girl was Margaret Bacon aged 9. She was alive but had appalling injuries. Dr Spencer did what he could but Margaret died of her injuries. He called for his colleagues and his medical bag and began treating the other children.

Seven year Ethel Kemp was brought in with a fractured leg. Dr. Spencer set that and left her to recover as he attended to the others.

There were no splints or bandages at the station so a parasol was broken to make splints, and handkerchiefs were used as dressings.

Later it was discovered that Margaret's older brother Joseph aged 10 had also been killed. Arthur Bacon the six year old younger brother had been with Margaret and Joseph at the Carr Vale Hall attending a Christmas party and film. He had not been with them at the crossing as he was the victim of torment from some other children and had tried to avoid them. Unbeknown, his tormenters had probably saved the young boy's life and his parents from losing all three children.

The third fatality that day was George Alfred Boot aged 8 who died of horrific injuries.

Mr. Breedon was killed on the same crossing the previous year. Curiously this man spent a great deal of time at the crossing and helping children cross in safety.

Ethel Kemp recovered from her injuries as did Arthur Yeats, aged 9 and John James Buxton aged 11.

Several ideas were put forward as to how this could be prevented from happening again including a subway, different kinds of gates, but the subway was finally decided on. A song was composed by Mr. E.M.Smith, a blind Evangelist from Sheffield. Below and overleaf are the first two verses and chorus.

One Christmas Eve those children so gay,
Had been to the pictures and were coming away;
They waited a moment for one train to pass,
They saw not the goods train coming so fast.

CHORUS
Looking this way, yes, looking this way,
Those little darlings are looking this way;
Sufferings are over, so happy are they,
In Heaven with Jesus and looking this way.

One little boy so happy and brave,
Held the hand of his sister with smiles on his face;
He'd just gained a prize for singing so sweet,
He's now with the angels in yond golden street.

He titled the song; '*At Peace with Jesus*'

1923 ACCIDENT AT BOLSOVER STATION

Eight year old Herbert Hayes was returning home from school one Wednesday in October 1923 with his friends. They were playing on the railway and waited on the embankment for a goods train from Chesterfield to pass. They then decided to rush across and were hit by a ballast train coming from the opposite direction. Herbert was hit by the train and killed instantly, his friend Leonard Platts aged 8 sustained serious injuries but survived.
Although the subway at this time was in use, the boys decided to climb the gate and run across the tracks.

Fig 35 Plaque in the memorial garden at Carr Vale

. It was a fatal error for Herbert. Mr.Haddock, the local Headmaster had warned his pupils several times.
A memorial plaque now stands on the site of the tragedies. *(see fig 35)*

THE MIDLAND RAILWAY

On 1st September 1890 The Midland Railway opened 'Bolsover Station', *(see fig 36 and 37)* later to be renamed 'Bolsover Castle Station' so as not to confuse it with the Lancashire, Derbyshire and East Coast Railway station at Carr Vale, which was also called Bolsover station. That was also renamed as Bolsover South.

Fig 36

The Midland station at Bolsover stood at the bottom of Station Road across from was what later to become Bolsover Colliery.
The line was known as the 'Doe Lea Branch', basically as most of its length ran along the river of the same name.

Fig 37

The initial idea for the line was authorised back in 1863. Several amendments and alterations were submitted, and after seventeen years the station, together with the other two stations on the line was opened.

The other two stations at that time as the train left Bolsover were, Palterton and Sutton then Rowthorne and Hardwick.

Palterton was a small single platform station situated on the south side of Carr Lane roughly between the villages of Palterton and Sutton Scarsdale. The lane was raised to allow a bridge to be built over the tracks.

Rowthorne again was a single platform station. The track then joined the main line and travelled through Pleasley and beyond.

Also to the left of the line approximately half a kilometre from Palterton station were sidings so bricks from the Bathhurst Brickyard could be loaded. Three trains per day ran each way initially and it was not until 1922 that extra services were added. As a result of local campaigning, a further station at Glapwell was opened in 1892. Up until then it was purely a platform for colliers.

The line closed to passenger traffic in 1930 but was still used by four local pits, the brickyard which by that time was called Byron Bricks and the Coalite. Ramcroft colliery closed in 1966 and Glapwell in 1974 but the track was not lifted immediately although it was redundant.

Some 'specials' were laid on by local organisations such as a trip to Cleethorpes on Sunday 13th August 1978 by Bolsover Miners' Welfare and several throughout the eighties.

With the closure of both Markham and Bolsover collieries in the 1990s, plus the Coalite going into receivership in 2004 the line was totally redundant along its length.

The tracks are long gone and very little remains. From the site of the old Bolsover colliery a track is still down running towards Staveley.

Running north from the colliery along the route of the railway is the Stockley Trail.

The Stockley Trail began in 1993 as part of the land reclamation project of the former Bolsover south spoil heaps. It now runs for over two miles and gives access to both the Carr Vale Nature Reserve and the Peter Fidler Reserve.

Views along the Stockley Trail taken by the Author:

The trains would go under several of these bridges on their way to Palterton and Sutton station, then beyond to Glapwell and Pleasley. Some of the rail track is still in place which ends at the beginning of the trail.

Looking back towards Bolsover Colliery

The end of the line, where the trail begins its journey towards Pleasley and beyond.

COAL MINING IN BOLSOVER

Coal is a natural resource which began its metamorphic journey around 300 million years ago. At that time the area which is now Bolsover was extremely wet and swampy. Vegetation died over time and created a layer of peat. *(see fig 38)* Over the millions of years that followed, sediment covered the peat, and the enormous pressure and weight caused tremendous heat which eventually turned the material into coal.

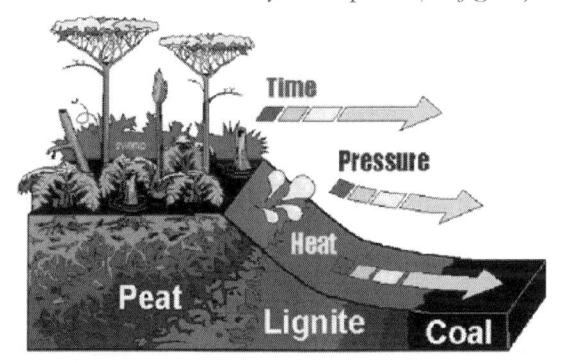

Fig 38

The Chinese were known to have used coal over 10,000 years ago and the Bronze Age people of Britain also saw its potential around 3,000 years ago. But it wasn't until the late 18th and early 19th centuries that coal came into the fore. The industrial revolution brought with it new machines, machines which ran on steam and could literally undertake the work of hundreds of human workers.

To produce steam, heat is needed, and at that time the best source of heat was coal. In the early 1800s steam locomotion was beginning to get a foothold in society. 1804 saw an Englishman, Richard Trevithick, build a full scale locomotive in South Wales *(see fig 39)*. The race was on to build bigger and more powerful engines. By 1829 George Stevenson won the Rainhill Trials with his now famous 'Rocket' *(see fig 40)*. Coal was big business, it warmed the home, it was in huge demand for industry so more collieries had to be constructed.

Fig 39 Trevithick's Loco 1804

Fig 40 below, Stevenson's Rocket 1829

In 1881 two local men, Josiah Court, a Surgeon from Staveley and William Mannikin, a mining engineer from Bolsover, took out a lease on land adjacent to where Carr Vale now stands and Bathurst Main Colliery was conceived. A rare early map shows the site of two shafts several hundred metres to the north of Bathurst main. It is unclear as to what these workings actually were. Bathurst or 'Batties' Main was on the south side of what was later the railway. Batties' was tough going from the onset. The two seams of coal called, Wales and Highmain (Also known as the Upper Silkstone and Silkstone seams) were difficult to mine due to their thickness. The Highmain seam was les only half a meter in places and the Wales was only 40 cm. The output of the colliery was small and soon became non viable. After several takeovers Bathurst Main finally closed in 1891.

Two years prior to the closing of 'Batties', in 1889, Emerson Muschamp Bainbridge *(See fig 41 below left)* founded the Bolsover Colliery Company. He obtained a lease from William Cavendish-Bentinck, 6th Duke of Portland *(see fig 42)*, to mine the 'Tophard' or 'Barnsley' coal beneath 8,000 acres of land in Derbyshire and Nottinghamshire. Bainbridge was born in Newcastle on Tyne in 1845 and educated at Doncaster and Durham University. In 1870 he became manager of Sheffield and Tinsley Collieries. He was also on the board of directors of the Lancashire, Derbyshire and East Coast Railway.

Fig 41 Emerson Bainbridge

Fig 42 6th Duke of Portland

The sinking of the shaft at Bolsover began in June 1890 with a twelve man crew, who finally hit the Top Hard in September 1891 at a depth of 334 meters and 1.9 meters thick.

It was normal in that era of sinking mines to set up brick making facilities nearby. At least two were known in Bolsover. One was east of the Midland railway track close to Palterton Station, and called Bathurst Brickyard, later Byron Bricks. The other was to service the new sinking of the shaft at Bolsover.

According to old maps, *(the map on the following page clearly shows the*

51

site of the brick works) it seems to have been on the east side of the colliery where the later area offices were built.

Bainbridge appointed a manager by the name of John Plowright Houfton. *(see fig 43).* Houfton was born in Chesterfield on December 13th 1857. He was educated at Eastwood National School and at Mr. Slater's Private School in Eastwood. He gained his Certificate as Colliery Manager in 1881.

Mr. J. P. Houfton.

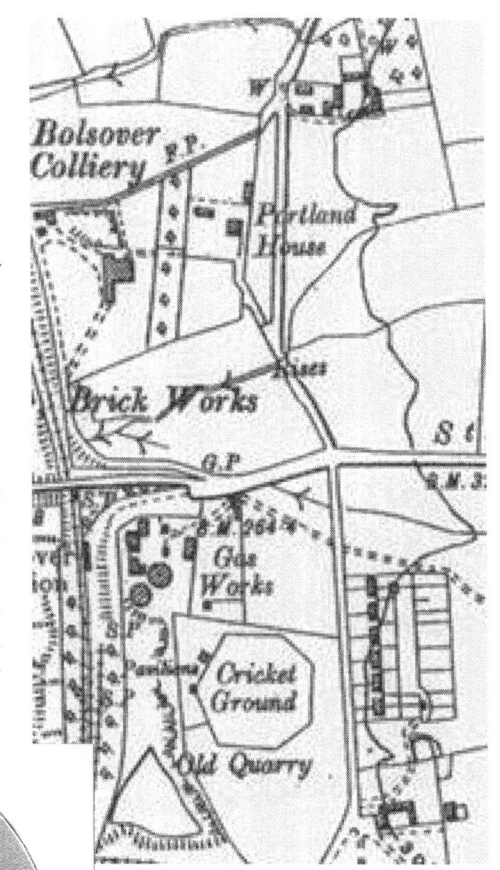

Fig 43 J.P.Houfton

He was manager of collieries in Manchester and Stoke-on-Trent before taking the post of General Manager of the Bolsover Colliery Company Ltd. in February 1890. He oversaw the shaft sinking at both Bolsover and Creswell Collieries. He went on to be the Chairman of Bolsover Urban District Council. Houfton took a keen interest in the welfare of the miners and their families. With the blessing of Bainbridge he put forward a vision of building homes and a social structure for the work force. He enlisted his architect cousin, Percy Bond Houfton *(see fig 44)* to submit plans for a 'Model Village' to be constructed a few hundred meters north east of the colliery. It was to consist of 200 houses, a Miner's Institute, school, co-operative store and an orphanage for children of miners who had been killed. Also Methodist and Anglican Churches, a bandstand in the centre of the green and allotments for the miners to grow produce. The final plans were submitted by a Nottingham firm of Architects, Brewill & Baily. A similar scheme on a larger scale was designed by Percy Houfton at Creswell.

Mr. P. B. Houfton.
Fig 44 P.B.Houfton

Building began in 1891 and a year later fifty of the two hundred houses were occupied.

Three types of houses were constructed in what is known as New Bolsover.

Single storey houses for 'small' families and double storey with attic rooms for 'larger' families. These were built in an inner and outer 'U' shape (see left plan).

School at New Bolsover

53

The third type were built nearer to the colliery and consisted of substantial dwellings known as the 'Villas' for housing the colliery officials.

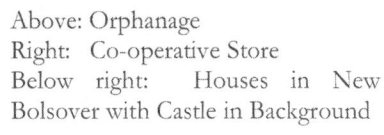

Above: Orphanage
Right: Co-operative Store
Below right: Houses in New Bolsover with Castle in Background

As can be seen from the above right photograph, a tramway system was used to take away the house hold rubbish and each miner received free coal. With the Railways, brickyards and coalmines; came the workers. Population increased dramatically and extra houses were built in Carr Vale itself, but unemployment was practically zero. A strong community was growing.

By the late 1800s, British coal and in particular Bolsover coal was in big demand in Germany. A German industrialist Otto Alfred Müller decided to improve the transporting of 'Bolsover coal' and commissioned the Rostock Shipyards in Germany to build a special ship in 1908. The MS 'Gretchen Müller' carried 1700 tons of coal each trip from England to Hamburg.

By 1895 output at Bolsover colliery had reached 1,800 tons per day and employing around 850 men. In 1905 this figure had reached 2,850 tons per day and in 1906 exported 300,000 tons from the mine.

Bolsover coal was said to be the finest coal in Europe and by 1923 the Bolsover Company was producing 11,000 tons per day. Some other pits in the Derbyshire coalfield began to run at a loss during the years between the two world wars, but Bolsover remained profitable. The company was able to modernise older pits and even develop new ones in North Nottinghamshire.

The opening of the Coalite works next to the colliery in 1936 was seen as a means to provide 'prosperity and contentment' of the community for years to come.

By 1935 miners no longer had to go home to bathe after a day underground as pit head baths were installed. In 1944 Bolsover colliery began to use a machine called the 'Gloster Getter' developed by V.W.Sheppard, formally of the Bolsover Company. This was a machine that could basically cut coal and transport it on conveyor belts to the shafts without pausing. It doubled the output per man-shift. This technique which was actually pioneered at Bolsover became known as the 'Bolsover System' and reduced the cost of producing coal considerably.

Bolsover employed around 1,000 men in 1956 and was producing 10,000 tons of coal per week.

Although coal 'reserves' were nationalised in 1942 during the Second World War, the mines themselves remained in private hands. The government set up the Coal Industry Nationalisation Act in 1946 and finally took over the mines on 'vesting day', 1st January 1947 at a cost of £338 million which would be well in excess of £12 billion in 2013.

1972 saw the first miner's strike since 1926. The National Union of Mineworkers (NUM) asked for a 43% pay increase. The National Coal Board offered around 8%. This was rejected by the NUM and action was taken.

The 'strength and unity' of Britain's workers began to take a toll on the country. Dockers refused to unload coal, picket lines were present at power stations, Docks, transport depots and all major fuel suppliers. ON the 9th February, a state of emergency was declared and a three day working week was implemented to save electricity.

An agreement was reached and the miners returned to work on 28th February 1972.

In late 1973 the Conservative Government had tried to introduce pay freezes and in some cases actual cuts. The miners had slipped from being the highest paid industrial workers to eighteenth. They decided once more to request a pay rise, the request was rejected. So on 9th February 1974 the miners came out on strike once again. The Prime Minister Edward Heath once again declared a state of emergency and a three day week. Heath called a General Election and was defeated, the incoming Labour Government and the miners reached a deal shortly after taking office.

The new Labour Secretary of State for Employment, Michael Foot implemented the Pay Board Report which showed how miner's pay had dropped since 1972.

The 1974 strike which was more low key than in 1972 produced not only an increase in pay, but implemented a scheme for compensation for pneumoconiosis sufferers. A new superannuation scheme was agreed and commenced in 1975.

During the strikes, the old Batties Main colliery site was 'unofficially' re-worked by striking miners. An upturned motor cycle was said to have been 'ingeniously' used to mechanise the extraction of the coal.

ERASIPTERON BOLSOVERI

(Gracefully Winged of Bolsover)

In 1978, Malcolm Spencer was walking along the Deep Hard Seam in Bolsover Colliery when he noticed something 'odd' in the roof of the mine workings. He wrapped it up and brought it topside. He placed the bag in his locker and contacted his friend Terry Judge who was known to be a fossil enthusiast by his friends. Finally, after threats by Malcolm that he would throw it away, Terry looked at it and immediately knew it was something special. He eventually sent it to the mine Geologist who photographed it and sent it to the Regional Geologist. Via the Institute of Geological Sciences it then went to Dr Paul Whalley, a specialist at the British Museum (Natural History).

Two years later it was officially declared a new species and called it Erasipteron Bolsoveri which translated means *'Gracefully winged of Bolsover.'*

It had a 20cm wingspan and was larger than anything found previously in the United Kingdom. Soon the world was interested in Malcolm's dragonfly. When coal was forming three hundred million years ago this dragonfly would have been trapped in amber and preserved for all time. Malcolm was offered the choice as finder to name the specimen. Rather than use his own name he unselfishly decided to honour the colliery and the town of Bolsover.

THE END OF COAL MINING

The decline of coal mining in Bolsover set in shortly after the 1984 miner's strike. A Conservative government was back in power and had learned many lessons from the strikes of 1972 and 1974. They had been preparing for such an event for ten years. Margaret Thatcher had backed off once in 1981 after action was threatened to stop sweeping pit closures. She would not do so a second time. Between 1981 and 1984, 40 pits had either been closed or merged.

Arthur Scargill was elected NUM President in December 1981. Although he won by a huge majority, the miners rejected a NUM proposal to strike over pay in 1982. In October 1982, 61% of miners again voted not to take strike action over pay, despite a campaign by Scargill to do so.

Even though action had been taken in Wales and Yorkshire over pit closures, the majority of NUM members still refused to strike. Ian MacGregor, the new Chairman of the Coal Industry began to pour fuel on the fire by announcing further pit closures.

Unlike the previous strikes in the seventies, the miners this time were divided. Some areas voted for action others like Leicester were 90% against action. The NUM was rapidly approaching its centenary. It was established in 1888 as the Miner's Federation of Great Britain and at that time was affiliated to the Labour party. But still it could not unite all the miners, the strike did not start on a set day as it had in previous strikes; it was a series of individual actions. On 12th March Scargill declared that the strikes in the various coal fields were to be a national strike and called all members to strike.

The strike finally ended on 3rd March 1985, nearly one year after it had began. Many members; however had returned to work for various reasons. A great deal of bad feeling had been generated. Bolsover was hit hard as Bolsover and surrounding collieries were a major employer in the town. Families struggled with even the basic of standards. The town had, although not as bad as some coal fields such as Yorkshire, been divided. Even families to this day have no interaction or communication with once loved ones.

By 1987 only 750 employees worked at Bolsover colliery, dropping to 600 only three years later. The local economy suffered another blow when in 1987 the area offices of British Coal closed.
When Bolsover colliery finally close in 1993 there were 350 employees.
To add further to the unemployment situation in Bolsover, the Coalite plant adjacent to Bolsover colliery, which, in 1972 employed over 1,200, went into receivership in 2004 with the loss of 350 jobs.

Bolsover and its long standing tradition of coal production was no more. The population had increased from a mere 2,000 in the 1800s to 11,000 solely on the advent of coal, railways, brick making and other industry. None of which now remain.

SUTTON SCARSDALE HALL

The present 18th century building is believed to be the fifth structure on the site. The original hall was on the estate owned by Wulfric Spott, he was an Anglo Saxon nobleman who died around 1002. Upon his death he left the estate to Burton-on-Trent Abbey which he had re-founded as a Benedictine abbey. In the Domesday Book of 1086 the estate was owned by Roger de Poitou. By 1225, King Henry lll gave the title, Lordship of Sutton-in-the-Dale to Peter de Hareston.

Around 1401 the estate had been purchased or inherited through marriage by John Leeke (Leke) of Cotham. It is quite possible that John Leeke was in fact Sir Simon Leeke mistakenly named John as at the time he took possession of Sutton and its estates he would have been around 26 years old. He did have a son called John who was born in 1400. The dates seem to be consistent with Simon having possession and obviously, his son John would have inherited the estate from his father. At some point the spelling of the name changed from Leeke or Leke to Leake.

Francis Leake (also known as Leak) was knighted in 1601 after being the Sherriff in 1586 and again in 1604 after his knighthood. Francis had a son called Francis. At that time the Leake family was one of the largest landowners in the Scarsdale Hundred of Derbyshire with other properties around Derbyshire and Nottinghamshire.

Francis senior was not a charitable neighbour. He seemed to be a ruthless landlord and was constantly bombarding the courts with requests, Chancery and common pleas. So much so that the Privy Council was persuaded to intervene to seek a 'final and neighbourly end' to all the litigation.

He was a difficult man and frequently quarrelled with other landlords including his cousin Henry Leake of Codnor.

When he died, his son Francis by his first wife inherited the estate and became Earl of Scarsdale in 1645.

Francis Leake, like William Cavendish came out for the Royalists and pledged to fight for Charles. He strengthened the structure of the hall considerably against attackers. Sir Francis defended the Hall several times as Parliamentary forces continued in their quest to take it, he had lost two sons in the war already and was determined to defend his estates. Colonel Sir John Gell, Commander in Chief of Parliamentary forces in Derbyshire, Staffordshire and Warwickshire, led a force of 500 Parliamentary troops against Sutton Scarsdale. Although Gel fought for the Parliamentarians, his loyalty was in question, so much so that after the war he was imprisoned for offering to give Charles 1 £900 after being found guilty of 'misprison of treason', that is to say he knew of a royalist plot but did not disclose it to the authorities.

Parliamentary forces finally took the hall and began systematically looting it. Sir Francis was fined £18,000 by Oliver Cromwell for his support for The Royalists. Friends helped him pay the fine and he began to restore the hall which had been left in a poor condition due to lack of maintenance. His sons Edward and Charles had been killed in the war as mentioned, and with his son Francis being killed in France, the estate went to his fourth son Nicholas 2nd Earl of Scarsdale.

Sir Nicholas Leake or Leke married Lady Frances Rich, daughter of the Earl of Warwick and had seven children, with Robert, the eldest succeeding his titles. Not only was Robert the 3rd Earl of Scarsdale, he was styled Lord Deincourt from 1655 to 1681. He was also a Captain in Lord Gerard's Regiment of Horse from 1678 to 1679. He had a brief career in politics by becoming MP for Newark in 1679.

He died in 1707 childless therefore his titles passed to his nephew Nicholas. The 4th Earl decided to renovate Sutton Scarsdale Hall so asked Warwick architect Francis Smith to transfer the hall to a Georgian style to rival the likes of Chatsworth.

The best craftspeople were employed including Francesco Vassalli from the Lugano district of Italy, who was at that time was believed to be one of the finest stucco plasterers in the world. Also the Atari brothers much sought after and famous stuccoists. Together with the Scottish neoclassical architect, interior designer and furniture designer Robert Adam, famed for his wonderful fire surrounds, they set to work and created a masterpiece to rival other, much larger mansions.

The Entrance Hall

Carved Adam fireplaces in Marble and Blue John, coupled with magnificent plaster work and mahogany staircase gave must have gone beyond Sir Nicholas's wildest expectations. Sir Nicholas never married and died in 1736 leaving the title Earl of Scarsdale extinct. Sometime between 1736 and 1740 Godfrey Bagnall Clarke purchased the estate. Ownership was then transferred through marriage to the Marquis of Ormonde. In the Royal Kalendar, and Court and City Register for England a Walter Butler, Lord Butler, is cited as Colonel of the Kilkenny Militia, Marquis of Ormonde in Ireland and Sutton Hall in 1801.

Following the death of the Marquis in 1824, the Hall was bought by Richard Arkwright Junior, the son of Sir Richard Arkwright of Cromford Mill fame. When Arkwright died in 1843 at the age of 88, he was reported to be the richest 'commoner' in England, and Sutton was passed to his son Robert. He married the actress Frances Crawford Kemble in 1805 much to the displeasure of his family. But eventually Frances warmed the hearts of all she met becoming a charming host and making friends with the aristocracy.

When Robert died in 1859, Sutton was passed to his son, the Reverend Godfrey Harry Arkwright. He had two marriages and produced three children by each, and it was his eldest son Francis who inherited the Hall after the Reverend's death in 1866.

In 1882 Francis decided to go to New Zealand and left Sutton Scarsdale Hall in the care of his cousin William Arkwright. William then inherited the property in 1915 as Francis had no male heir.

William decided to auction the Hall in 1919 with the rest of the estate.

The estate was bought by a group of local businessmen who immediately set about asset-stripping it. Much of it was shipped to the United States. The newspaper tycoon William Randolf Hurst bought much of the oak panelling for his ambitious residence in California called Hurst Castle. The panelling however, was simply stored in New York for many years until Pall Mall films bought it and used it on several film sets in the 1950s. Other panels are on display in the Philadelphia Museum of Art. The rest of the building was stripped, including the roof and sold off. By now the once grand Hall was nothing more than a shell, open to the elements and vandals. It was decided that due to the dangerous condition of the crumbling brickwork that it would be demolished. Upon hearing of this in 1946 Sir Osbert Sitwell of nearby Renishaw Hall purchased it to simply preserving the ruins.

As one walks around the ruins of Sutton Scarsdale Hall, it's hard to imagine that less than one hundred years ago this once fine example of Georgian architecture was actually a residence. There is an air of sadness in visitors as they contemplate would could have been.

Staircase and Hallway, Sutton Scarsdale Hall

63

Oak room showing portrait of Mrs Robert Arkwright.

The ruins of Sutton Scarsdale Hall.

OXCROFT SETTLEMENT

Although coal mining, together with the Coalite plant, dominated the local economy of Bolsover for a great deal of the 20th century, farming was still a vital activity in rural parts.

In February 1936, Derbyshire County Council approached Victor Christian William Cavendish, 9th Duke of Devonshire in an attempt to buy 399 acres of land north of Bolsover. The aim was to create an estate of smallholdings designed to alleviate some of the unemployment problems in industrial areas. It was hoped that unemployed men would be approached and vetted as to their suitability to undertake working on the land thus alleviating the dole queues. This was to be the only project of its kind in Derbyshire, and one of only two in England initiated by a county council (the other was at Duxbury in Lancashire).

Once the land had been purchased it was divided into 40 smallholdings of between four and a half and six acres each.
Below is a typical smallholding at Oxcroft.

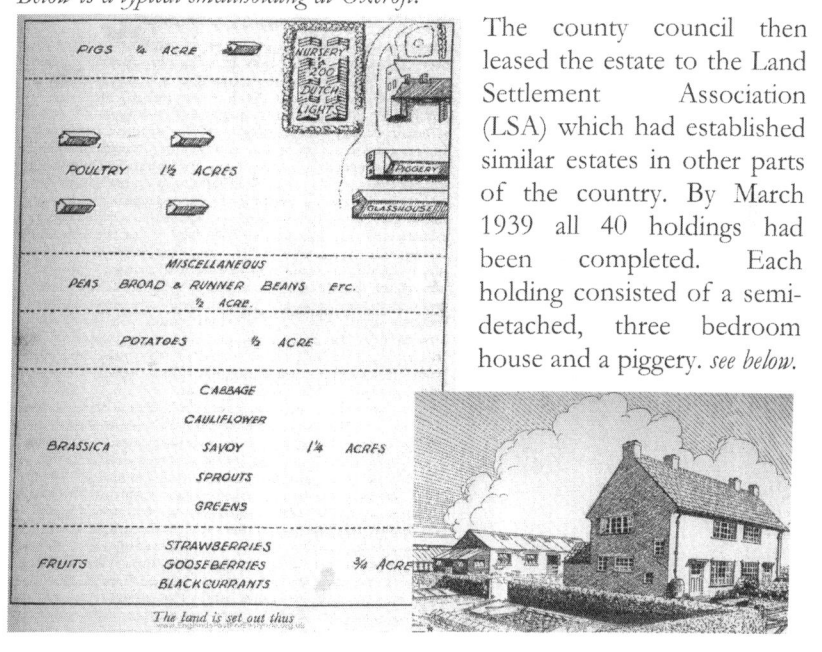

The county council then leased the estate to the Land Settlement Association (LSA) which had established similar estates in other parts of the country. By March 1939 all 40 holdings had been completed. Each holding consisted of a semi-detached, three bedroom house and a piggery. *see below.*

65

By 1939, 37 families had been settled. Some men were familiar with working the land but 20 were undergoing training at the time.

Although each holding had around 5 acres, one acre was allotted for top fruit, i.e. strawberries, Gooseberries etc: and two acres for market gardening such as cabbage, cauliflower, sprouts etc. The remaining area would be devoted as a piggery. Each household had two sows and 30 baconers (a pig usually between 83 and 101kg at market).

Also several greenhouses were erected around the settlement and in some cases the existing old farm buildings were utilised. The remaining land was retained as a 'Central Farm' or 'Estate Service Depot' and was overseen by the Estate Manager.

(Estate Manager Area)

The scheme was innovative in its conception but was met with some scepticism by many who were approached. At report from the time stated that when the scheme was explained to 'a large gathering of unemployed' at Chesterfield there followed a 'lively discussion and some criticism'. However, 105 applicants were received for the 40 tenancies. In March 1936 the first batch of would be farmers arrived including miners, ex-military men, labourers, electricians, a grocer, a stone mason and even a basket maker.

The men lived alone on the settlements as their training progressed and were joined by their families once they were deemed proficient enough to commence farming without supervision.

In October 1936 the (UAB) Unemployment Assistance Board questioned in some cases the recruitment of certain of the men at Oxcroft believing that they had come from parts of Derbyshire not designated as 'depressed'.

The UAB and the Ministry finally agreed that a few men could be drawn from other areas, but the coalfield would be the main source of labour.

The tenants, although they had completed their training were still given support and advice from the estate manager. During the Second World War the aim of the scheme was disrupted as resettling unemployed workers gave a back seat to maximising food output.

Tenancies were strictly regulated to men who had farming backgrounds. The number of pigs was reduced as too many storage buildings were being used to house feed etc. The number of tenancies fell to 26, but reports stated that those families were, 'breezy and happy people with bright and healthy children; a striking contrast to the 'depressed and delicate' group who had arrived in early 1936. The tenants were producing food on a large scale and in some cases returning £400 in 1942.

Left: Picking onions on Oxcroft Settlements

After the Second World War the Ministry of Agriculture took over responsibility for the Land Settlement Association and wrote of its capital debts in return for the freehold of its estates. These included the two leased from Derbyshire and Lancashire county councils.

Oxcroft was acquired by the Ministry of Agriculture and Fisheries in 1951 A report in 1957 by the regional land commissioner stated that the farm buildings at Oxcroft were in fairly good condition despite subsidence and that the holdings were being well cultivated and put to good use. As modern farming and mass production methods improved it was becoming more and more difficult for tenants take make a living. As they left the settlements no new tenants took on the challenge and so the properties began to slowly succumb to time and

The community centre at Oxcroft

weather, and lack of maintenance. In 1962 the regional land agent reported that demand for tenancies remained slow and that some of the holdings were actually being farmed by the estate manager who was doing an excellent job. By 1963 the estate was described as 'untidy' and in 1965 only 23 of the 40 holdings were let.

There were only 17 holdings let by 1968 and the Ministry was seriously considering closing the estate and selling the land off. The NCB at the time was also interested in the land as it wished to opencast the site.

Another problem was pollution from the Coalite plant and Staveley works. A tomato crop had been rejected due to a 'taste' problem which was blamed on emissions from the Coalite.

With this final 'nail in the coffin' as it was described there was nothing the MAF could do, and so the estate lands and buildings were sold off.

Although the houses are now occupied by their owners, few are as they were in 1936. Piggeries are gone, outbuildings flattened and extensions and renovations to the houses have been undertaken. However, the area is still an area of outstanding beauty and tranquility. As one walks up Oxcroft Lane beyond the impeccably kept municipal cemetery the countryside surrounds you along the narrow lane. It's not too long before you see the first of the three bed roomed semis built in 1936 standing as proud as the day they were built. A fabulous view over the valley towards Sheffield and beyond almost demands that you stop and take in the vista.

Some small agriculture still takes place on the settlements but most are now private and much sought after dwellings.

HALIFAX BOMBER CRASH 1944

During the late evening of 21st March 1944, a Halifax bomber took off from RAF Dishforth in North Yorkshire. The Canadian 1664 Heavy Conversion Unit equipped with several of the four engine bombers were stationed there. The crew took the aircraft up on a training flight. The bomber, LK931 had been relegated to training flights only, due to its age.

69

The 'mission' was believed to be what was known as 'a nickel', this entailed dropping leaflets over occupied territory and in some instances even dropping thousands of metal strips called 'windows' or 'chaff' as it was called by the Americans. This was to confuse enemy radar.

The crew was relatively young except the Bomb Aimer, Russell Peel who at the age of 31 was referred to as 'Pop' by the others. The crew had been together for over four months but had never flown this particular route before. Peel recalled that approaching France they were ordered to return to base. As Sergeant Ray Collver, the pilot, turned the huge aircraft around 'something went violently wrong with the starboard outer engine'. It was unsure as to whether this had been caused by enemy action or a mechanical fault. Some of the crew did in fact see flashes from the ground which may have been anti aircraft fire. The operation was changed from dropping leaflets to 'a Bulls eye' which was a fake raid to lure German fighters from the main force. As they were within twenty minutes of RAF Dishforth, the engine began to vibrate so badly that paint to fall from the inside of the aircraft.

Wally Loucks, the Wireless Operator recalled. "The noises inside were like I imagined several large animals - dinosaurs fighting for their lives. The aluminium was falling like snow and I could hear Ray's (Ray Collver) voice yelling for us to hurry and get out"

The order to 'bale out' was given. By now the aircraft was ablaze and dangerously low but pilot Ray Collver stayed at the controls and tried to avoid any built up area. The bomber skimmed the trees as it flew from Mansfield towards Hillstown, Palterton and Scarcliffe. Three parachutes inflated and Ralph Pilkington, Wally Loucks and Russell Peel watched helplessly as Collver tried to level the bomber out for a crash landing. The aircraft 'belly flopped' into a field and its momentum took it across a road where it hit a high roadside bank. Had this bank not have been so high, the aircraft may have carried on into the next field. The

Flight Engineer and two gunners together with Collver were still on board at this time.

The pilot was thrown clear, but the remaining three crew members were trapped in the now blazing wreckage. Ralph Pilkington landed safely although he was hanging by his parachute from a lamp post.

Carl Starnes who was the rear gunner was trapped in the wreckage and his clothing was on fire. He was shouting for help and two local brothers braved the flames and exploding ammunition to douse his clothing and eventually pull him out. George and Albert Calow stripped the airman of his smouldering clothes once outside the bomber. Although both brothers were severely burned, Albert drove the young Canadian to Dr. McKay's house in Bolsover. Starnes was then transferred to Chesterfield Royal Hospital but sadly died of his injuries. The Calow brothers spent months recovering from the horrendous burns they had suffered while rescuing the airman.

The emergency services later recovered two bodies from the wreckage.

Several miles away, Bomb Aimer Russell Peel was found in a field and taken to Warsop Police Station. Wally Loucks and Ralph Pilkington were taken to King's Mill Hospital in Mansfield, which at that time was an American Military Hospital.

It was not until March 2000 that a stone with a brass plaque was erected on the site by an anonymous local donor.

The two Calow brothers were awarded the 'British Empire Medal' for their outstanding bravery in attempting to save the life of the Canadian airman.

The pilot, who later became Reverend Ray Collver returned to the site years after and met Albert Calow whose brother George had died previously. He preached a service at Mansfield Woodhouse Church before returning home.

Handley Page Halifax. Introduced in 1940, over 6,000 were built and remained in service until 1961 when several were sold to the Pakistani Air Force

PETER FIDLER

Born in Bolsover on 16th August 1769, Peter Fidler signed on as a labourer for the Hudson Bay Company at the age of 19. Once in Canada, he began his training as a surveyor under the supervision of Philip Turnor. (This spelling is sometimes disputed as being Turner) He was an outstanding map maker to the extent several of his maps are still in use today. Peter worked with David Thompson *(see bottom left)* in Canada. Thompson was reported to be 'The greatest land geographer who ever lived'. Like Peter, he was an Englishman and studied under Turnor. While at Cumberland House, Saskatchewan, Thompson had an accident in December 1788 and fractured his leg. Turnor had organised an expedition of exploration to the west attempting to find a route to the Pacific Ocean. This gave Peter an opportunity to accompany his tutor on the expedition. In 1790 the team set off to spend the next two years heading west. Peter gathered data and produced several detailed maps of the areas visited. Over the coming years he was so well respected that he established further settlements including: Carlton House Saskatchewan in 1795, and Chesterfield House in 1800. He also established Bolsover House near Meadow Lake in Saskatchewan in 1797.

Fidler had 14 children, 3 of whom died in infancy. Mary Mackegonne, his wife was a Cree Indian, a native of Canada. She was his lifelong companion and travelled with his during his explorations.

Peter's father James was a constable, a miller and a farmer. He was born in Sutton Mill Farm *(see above)* on what is now the A632 Bolsover to Chesterfield road. He had one brother James Jr., who was a road surveyor, and a sister Sarah.

In September of 1819, Peter took charge of Fort Dauphin near Winnipegosis in Manitoba with his son Charles, who was now a company employee. At 50 years old, illness began to creep in and during the winter of 1820 - 21 he was 'attacked with Palsy' in that he was beginning to suffer paralysis and tremors. He died on December 17, 1822 at Fort Dauphin.

There are few images of Peter, whether he was a modest man and shy of his own image no one can say, but tributes to him have been erected on the two continents. Previous page is the famous statue at Elk Point in Alberta on Highway 41. It is 10 meters high by 2 and a half meters wide. It was carved with a chain saw by Herman Poulin. There is also a stone monument in Meadow Lake, Saskatchewan.

But of course right here in Bolsover, Peter has a whole nature reserve dedicated to him including a commemorative stone cairn similar to his memorial at Dauphin in Canada.

Below and overleaf are images of the Peter Fidler Nature Reserve taken by the Author.

One of many pathways above, each one leading to spectacular views of the reserve and surrounding countryside.

Below: showing Bolsover Castle commanding the view over the nature reserve.

THE KNIGHTS HOSPITALLER

The Knights Hospitaller, also known as Knights of Saint John (which is where the present day organisation gets its name) amongst other titles was among the most famous of the Western Christian military orders during the middle ages. It is believed that old documents relate to an area in Bolsover called Spittal Green which was the site of a hospital. The document states that there was a small hospital with few material assets, but little else is known.

At that time the Knights Hospitallers set up small hospitals to treat and give rest to pilgrims travelling between various local Abbeys and Churches. It would also have probably been a guest house for returning nights having fought in the crusades. The Hospitallers set up these establishments and run them as charitable organisations relying of donations and gifts to look after the sick and elderly.

It is known that the hospital was still at Spittal Green in 1485 due to a document which states that the hospital at Bolsover is of lesser class than those found elsewhere in the country. It was most probably dissolved in the early sixteenth century. As other similar hospitals in Barlborough, Staveley and Chesterfield were of a better standard.

THE CHANGING FACE OF BOLSOVER

From the two maps below and overleaf (roughly to the same scale), it is hard to comprehend the magnitude of change in the area over the years. The top map is from a study in 1835, in itself not ancient history. It is evident that there is no Carr Vale, save for perhaps a few cottages. No Hillstown, named after Mr. Hills and the streets named after his sons. The housing estate along Moor lane was still fields in 1935. The Castle estate, New Bolsover and even the railways, were all still visions of what was to come. The population rose in the century following the top map, from around 2,000 to the 12,000 plus it is now, and is still growing with the building of more and more new housing.

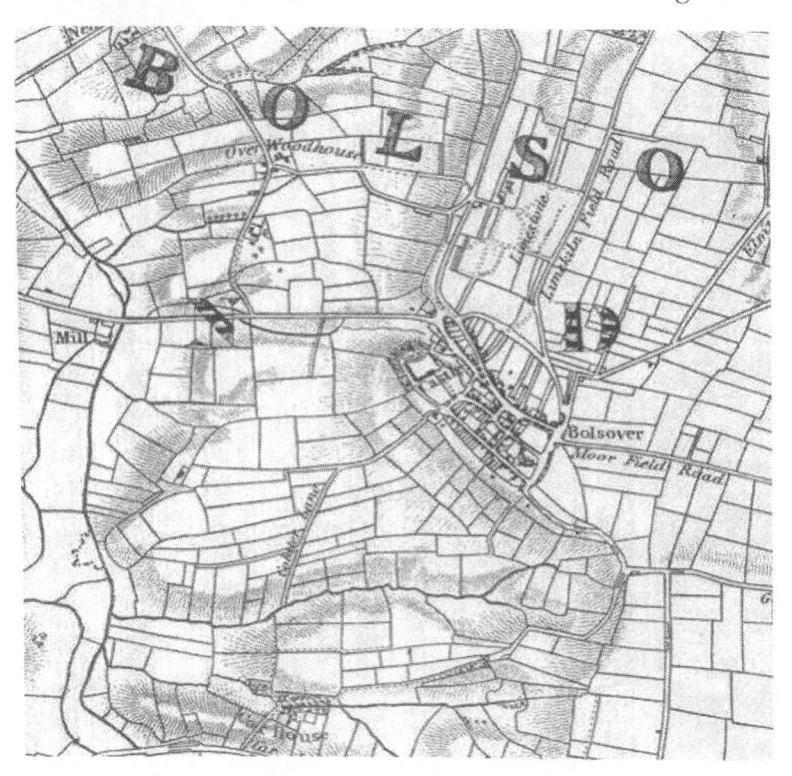

Below are two photographs taken from roughly the same spot almost a century apart. They are of Charlesworth Street in Carr Vale.

Up until the Railways, Pits and Brick Works, Carr Vale was little more than a hamlet leading from Bolsover down Cobster Lane through the village and onto Carr Lane leading to Carr Farm. *(left)* which was demolished in the 1960s. Below are three very different views of Main Street Carr Vale. Left showing the Carr Vale Hotel and on the right as it is in 2013, a convenience store.

Moving on up the hill to the start of Castle Lane stands a care home on the site of the only

80

swimming baths in Bolsover. *The picture of Bolsover baths on previous page shows construction in 1925).*

The baths were built in 1925 and held many functions aside from swimming. The pool would be boarded over and dances held, often until the early hours of the morning. It was deemed too costly to maintain and was finally closed in 1990. As of 2013, despite continued action from devoted residents, no plans have been finalised for its replacement.

Still further up and taking the right road called New Station Road are several places on the left where a fault line was detected in the magnesium limestone. This area is locally known as the 'Back Hills'.

Once at the top of New Station Road, the true magnificence of the Doe Lea Valley can be appreciated. The ruin of Sutton Scarsdale Hall stands proudly on the opposite side of the valley. The river from which it takes its name meanders slowly from its beginnings in Hardwick, on through Staveley and beyond. From that vantage point the viewer looks over the site of the hospital on Spittal Green, now a housing estate and on to where the old Batties pit would have stood. Slightly to the right towards Carr Vale would have been the Station of the Lancashire, Derbyshire and East Coast Railway. One could watch the trains depart the station from this spot and see them disappear into the tunnel to emerge on the other side of the hill in Scarcliffe.

Also on a site adjacent to the station was a large building with goods loading bays and sidings. This was known locally as 'The Jam Factory'.

Left; Inside the 'Jam Factory'

In 1900 a company was set up calling itself the Bolsover Home Grown Fruit Preserving Company Ltd. The chairman was J.P.Houfton of the

Bolsover Colliery Company and other directors including three members of the Tinsley family, one of whom farmed 200 acres of fruit.

Percy Houfton designed the complex on a two and a half acre site adjacent to the Lancashire, Derbyshire and East Coast Railway station at Carr Vale to enabled goods to be transported by rail as well as road. One reason for this enterprise was to employ local women in a mining community such as Bolsover. In the early years most of the fruit was produced locally, in particular, strawberries; other fruit would come from Wisbech and the Fens mostly by rail. Canning played a part in the factory where it canned plums, apples, oranges and lemons from Liverpool docks and even peas and corned beef. With the decline in the demand for Jam and the lack of sufficient storage facilities, coupled with large conglomerates undercutting through bulk buying, the factory began to reduce until it ceased trading in 1959. The following year, the factory was acquired by the council for industrial development. The factory premises were later occupied by a business manufacturing lubricants.

Turning right and walking past the Hornscroft, further historical evidence would be evident by looking to the right to see remains of earthworks, which at one time would have encircled the town. A plaque explaining the Hornscroft and Dykes earthworks has been erected at the Town End side of the park. *(see above)*. Walking on towards High Street, the Parish Church of St. Mary and St. Laurence appears on the right hand side. The castellated square structure adjoining the main church is the Cavendish Chapel built in the 17th century. *(see picture below)*.

The Cavendish Chapel was built in 1618 and was designed by Huntingdon Smythson. It was to house a memorial to Sir Charles Cavendish and his wife Catherine Ogle.

Below: Inside the Cavendish Chapel Sir Charles Cavendish and his wife Catherine, Baroness Ogle.

Continuing along High Street, passing several of Bolsover's historical buildings, brings the visitor to a strange looking house at the very top of Castle Lane. Where Castle Lane becomes Castle Street, stands a 'Gothic' structure known locally as the 'Three penny bit' house. (*right*) St. Mary's or 'The School House' was built originally for the master of the infants' school adjacent, but over the years it was occupied by the various curates of the church. It is now a private dwelling. By the left hand side of the house can be seen a gateway. This gateway would have been the original entrance to the castle as guests and visitors made their way to the magnificent terrace. *(left)*

The Terrace with its long gallery and steps where carriages would have pulled up for guests to alight.

There is so much history to the town of Bolsover it would take several volumes to document it in its entirety.

Evidence of Bolsover's past can be found all around, even in the names of the streets for example: *(not in alphabetical order)*

Sutton Hall Road Road:

Scarsdale Street:

Bainbridge Road:

Spittal Green:

New Station Road: (From Bolsover to Carr Vale Station)

Houfton Road:

Peveril Road:

Cundy Road:

Welbeck Road:

Portland Avenue and Crescent:

Cavendish Road:

Nesbit and Selwyn Street: (Named after two sons of Mr. Hills)

Chatsworth Close:

Smithson and Huntingdon Avenues:

To name but a few.

History is all around us, for example, how often do we see a road sign and think "I wonder where that came from?" or the sign on a building saying 'Mill House' or 'The Old Rectory'. Many are purely self explanatory like; Limekiln Fields Road, Quarry Road and Crich View.

AND FINALLY

During the Second World War Lord Beaverbrook came up with a novel idea for towns across England to 'sponsor' a Spitfire. Bolsover rose to the challenge and bought not one, but two of our most famous fighter aircraft. A total of £11,400 was raised for the two. A feat of pride to this day as Chesterfield did not raise enough money for even one. The miners were fundamental in this exercise and gave one old penny for every ten shillings they earned. *(Ten shillings is equivalent to fifty pence today).*

Both Spitfires saw active service. They were the Spitfire Mk 1 built by Vickers Armstrong (Supermarine), and first flew in 1940. They were assigned 'Bolsover 1, R7261 and Bolsover 2, 7276.

7261 was based in Londonderry and served with the USAAF protecting American convoys coming across the Atlantic. The aircraft or the pilots seemed to be prone to accidents, firstly in September 1942 it flew into high tension cables, the pilot was not injured and the plane was repaired. In 1944 it tipped onto its nose whilst taxiing and again was repaired. It was then relegated to training and was finally struck off charge in 1947.

7276 was not so lucky and was shot down one mile south of Dungeness in September 1941. The pilot, Sergeant Cooper was killed and his body was found later. He now rests in Luton Cemetery.

85

Acknowledgements

Wikipedia
MBArchaeology Local Heritage Series
H.M.S.O.
University of Nottingham
Britannica
Railwaysarchive.co.uk
Oldminer.co.uk
Richardsbygonetimes.co.uk (Special thanks)
Englands Past For Everyone
Bolsover District Council

Also to the many residents, who have shared their stories and memories with me, and given me the incentive to produce this work.

I look forward to meeting with more wonderful people in researching the second 'Ripple in Time' book of the series.

I would be grateful to anyone who may be in possession of old photographs, news items and personal accounts to contact me. I thank you in anticipation of your kindness.

John.S.Haywood@Sky.Com

ISBN 978-1-291-64659-7

©2013 John Stuart Haywood

All information in this publication has been carefully researched, and where verification has not been possible, the author has taken the most popular account and cannot be held responsible for any errors or omissions.